# A Consultant's Devotional

## Alan D. Jones

RISING SUN GROUP PUBLISING
www.AlanDJones.com
Atlanta, Georgia, USA

# A Consultant's Devotional
By Alan D. Jones

Rising Sun Group Publishing
Copyright © 2021 Alan D. Jones

ISBN-13: 978-1-7344414-2-0
Library of Congress Control Number: Pending

**Notes:**

Cover Image: Alan Jones
Editing Services: Anika Jones, Yolanda Johnson, Alan Jones
Consulting Services: Eva Ruth Bird
Interior Page Layout & Design: Alan Jones
Front & Back Cover Design: Alan Jones

**Continue the conversation at:**
**www.theconsultantantsdevotional.com**

**Notes:**

# *Meditation/Reflection:*

*The purpose of this devotional is to facilitate thirty days of mediation and reflection, that each of us might find our own path, the one that our Creator set for each of us.*

*Thus, as you process through each day, please make note of anything that comes to your heart in the area provided.*

*Then after some time, take this thirty-day journey once again, and note what comes to mind during your second pass.*

*Then as you are led, walk this road once more, being sure to review your previous thoughts, and what the Lord shared with you the first two times you passed this way.*

*May the Good Lord bless each of you.*

*Sincerely, Alan*

**Notes:**

# Ticketing:

"Whatever you do, work at it with all your heart, as though working for the Lord." – Colossians 3:23

*When you try to help, they will question your motives, help anyway.*
*When you speak the truth, they will condemn you, speak the truth anyway.*
*When you aren't who they want you to be, be anyway.*
*It's not about being liked, being perfect or even being loved.*
*It's about allowing space, being authentic and being loving, anyway.*
*For you do not answer to them, but to the one you are becoming...*

Consider that when you're at a client site your assigned tasks can be difficult and quite complex, often times with no simple or easy solution. But at the end of the day, what you owe

**Notes:**

your client is your effort, your fealty and your experience. But from your soul's perspective, what you offer your client is a statement of who you are, rather than who you are to your client. For if we are people of faith, then it is our Creator whom we serve, and our calling to present in such a way to honor that call and the One who called us. A previous generation called this "guarding your witness." And although this is still true, if we take one step beyond that, we encounter another truth. That anyone despite our best efforts may rightly or wrongly find us lacking, and at times treat us unfairly. But regardless of how they may treat us, how we respond to them is a statement of who we are and who we serve.

Likewise, within every community or space in which we serve, we must remember Who we represent. In short, it's not about us having our way, but rather about us showing the Way, by how we behave and how we respond to difficult situations. Living our faith is not only a benefit to others, it is truly a benefit to us! As we strive to

**Notes:**

become more like our Redeemer, the joy we feel, knowing that we are walking in faith as best we can when we bow before the Lord each night, is priceless.  Not that we are prideful in our own deeds, but rather the joy we feel when we enter into the presence of the Almighty, laying bare all that we are, is without comparison.

**Notes:**

# Checking In:

"Therefore encourage one another and build each other up, just as you are doing."

1 Thessalonians 5:11

*I Apologize*

*for not reaching into your life*
*for not asking the question that really mattered*
*for not asking the next question*
*for not risking your condemnation*
*for leaving so much unsaid*
*for leaving so much undone*
*for not hearing your cry*
*for conforming to the expectations of this world, when I belong to another*

*I apologize for letting you go...*


In our all too busy lives, we must never forget to check in with those in our circle. We all know that project life can be all consuming at times. Outside of our immediate family, we can

**Notes:**

lose track of those second and third level connections; cousins, former co-workers and friends we've made along the way. We all too willingly assume that no news, is good news, when in fact, someone we care about may be struggling and could benefit from our assistance, even if it's only a kind word. This thin slicing of relationships beyond our immediate family is certainly a product of the demands on our time by our chosen profession. And it's not that we're afraid of bad news or requests for financial assistance. No, we're most afraid that reaching out to these outer layers of our world will require our most precious commodity, time.

But here's the thing that I've learned over the years. I've learned to trust the Spirit within. So, what does that mean? It means that when you do reach out to family and friends to check in with them, be fully present, listen without agenda and allow things to flow organically. One rule of thumb that I have, is that if doesn't adversely affect my relationship with God, family or those I love, I'm

**Notes:**

open to it. So yes, have your boundaries, they're important. But beyond your innate comfort zone; is a whole world which could benefit from your gifts.

**Notes:**

# Pre-flight:

"Cast all your anxieties on Him, because He cares for you." 1 Peter 5:7

*Truth only takes root in fertile ground.*

My God, I am humbled by thy faithfulness unto me.

A Prayer: *To the One who was, is and ever shall be, bless me with thy Holy Spirit, that I might have your peace and let go of all these earthly things. Let my thoughts be your thoughts, that I might serve your holy purpose. Indeed, may my life be a prayer unto You and a blessing unto Your creation.*

Repeat the following as you focus on your breathing: *"I let go of all these things, and give them over to You...".* Repeat as many times as needed.

The prayer above is one that I pray in the

**Notes:**

morning during times when I'm feeling stressed. If you've been in consulting for any amount of time, you've likely faced those days that challenge your resolve as well. Days when you awake knowing the weight of the tasks that await you, before you've even placed a second foot on the floor of your hotel room.  In those times, I say the prayer listed above, and at the end, I repeat "I let go of all these things, and give them over to you…" as I envision physically giving my burdens, concerns and fears over to the Lord at the Lord's holy altar. With each breath I release, I let go a little more as I repeat those words of release over and over, until I'm settled and ready for the day. In a very real sense, by doing this, I am preparing the ground for God's blessings to take root in my day and my life.

It is important that we not carry the burdens of the past into our present. For when we do, we weigh ourselves down, and delay the blessings that await us. Letting go of our burdens, past and present, allows us to prioritize and focus on those

**Notes:**

tasks that need our immediate attention. More importantly, letting go allows us a heavenly peace and a meditative state which aids us in hearing our Creator's voice throughout the day, and dare I say, throughout our lives.

**Notes:**

# Flight Delay:

"And we know that for those who love God all things work together for good, for those who are called according to his purpose." Romans 8:28

*Although.*

*My thoughts vacillate.*

*From times when I am adrift in a sea of numbness as the world spins around me, to other times possessing feelings of being broken beyond repair. Somehow, I thought there would be more. The lie creeps into my head that I should be more, despite the repeated counting of my many blessings.*
*What currents have brought me here, to this place of desolation and formlessness?*
*Was it the heartache the first time I saw my own reflection? Or was it written before my birth that I would be so?*

**Notes:**

*What manner of creature feels these things, much less expresses such longings back to its Creator?*

*Held captive in a prison of my own design, shackled by expectations planted long ago, by parties indifferent to my wellbeing, I am left wondering.*

*Still*

*My solace remains.*

*I strongly suspect that my own imperfections make me the perfect tool for my purpose in this life. Being set adrift to contemplate my existence is every bit what should be. It is who I am...*
*I am a buoy at sea offering a point of reference to those still ashore. And while the waves push me to and fro, I know there is a tether tied unto me, which will not yield when called upon. This is my faith, and I shall live and die by it, be I on the water or dry land. If you will step out unto the water to share this experience of uncertainty with me, you will get wet; there's no denying that. But know too that your fear anchors you to a lone spot on the shore, while faith sets you free upon the sea of possibilities. If you will hold my hand, I will hold yours and together we will experience the highs and lows of each passing wave.*

**Notes:**

*We shall be what we were meant to be, imperfect creatures bound by a perfect love.*

Despite our best planning and all of our good intent, sometimes things go wrong, crushingly so. For there is a universal truth for all flesh, things fall apart. The arc of entropy is the natural order of things. And yet, as human beings we struggle our entire lives for order. And as consultants, we're actually paid to make it so.

However sometimes, no matter how gifted we are, things go left. Sure, it's our job to be prepared and to speak truth to the client when they're asking for things that aren't realistic or wise. Still, if you're in the profession long enough, you will on occasion be asked to make a dollar out of fifteen cents. Seasoned consultants have all been there, and we've learned ways to mitigate downsides in such situations.

And still, despite all our experience and skill, there are times when the pendulum swings your way, and something in your life goes woefully

**Notes:**

wrong, and so much so that you feel defeated. Did your manager decide that you weren't a good fit? Were you over-weighted in equities the last time the market crashed? Did you hurt the one person you loved most in this world?

Bottomline, bad things happen. And when they do, we are left to ponder our whole existence, for in the moment, we sense a finality in these setbacks. And yet, they are very seldom the end of the story. From our Creator's perspective, they are merely commas in the stories of our lives. For every twist and turn, mold this clay pot into something glorious, someone destined for heaven.

**Notes:**

# Boarding:

"Suppose one of you wants to build a tower. Will you not first sit down and estimate the cost...?" – Luke 14:28

*As we search for our place in this life, as we work out our salvation, let us consider the nature of the destination we all seek. Then we will realize that the assurance of heaven is not a palace in the sky, but a peace within.*

As consultants we seek solutions and attempt to provide guidance to our clients. But on another level its deeper than that. What we really offer our clients is transformation. Thus, we must envision the destination (the future state), and then begin the process of developing a roadmap to get there.

Similarly, this is what our God offers to each

**Notes:**

of us. Rather than treasures on earth, what our Creator offers to us through the Holy Spirit, is to be transformed. And lest you think that the pursuit of Godly truth will somehow diminish our earthly joy, it will not. In fact, this quest we take on, will open our eyes to wonders previously unknown to us. The joy in this path will surpass all that we might find in the world. But it does come at a price. At the time this scripture was spoken, the cost was not only the giving up of earthly treasures, but quite possibly of one's own life. And though the latter is not a risk for most reading this, in some parts of the world, one's life may well still be the price. Here Jesus reminds us, even today, that anything of worth has a price, especially being His disciple. Choosing this path is the most important decision of a believer's life.

**Notes:**

# Take Off:

"Did God really say, 'you must not eat from any tree in the garden'?" – Genesis 3:1

*As the years stream by, I find that life is less about finding the right answers, than it is about asking the right questions. Energy spent chasing after answers to the wrong questions, can never be recaptured.*

The Bible story behind the quoted verse is about the rise of consciousness in humans and the corresponding awareness of good and evil. While it can be argued that we, as consultants, in many ways walk into a new client site, day one, much like Adam and Eve in the garden, not being sure of the players, nor their motives (Adam and Eve had been given clear instructions and yet they doubted). This can sometimes lead to the typical new person fail, of inadvertently stepping on company specific

**Notes:**

landmines. For instance, if you find that the client is not following an industry standard, and as the new consultant onsite, you suggest during the weekly status meeting that the client implement said process. And then to your surprise the director of said department states tersely, "No, we're not doing that." End of conversation. A seasoned consultant would have known that such findings should be vetted with a trusted client staffer, before ever being suggested to upper management in an open forum.

The same principle can be applied to life in general. It was unwise for the consultant to raise such a concern to the client for the first time in a room full of client suits. There are precursors, due diligence questions, which one should ask or at least think through, when addressing real world problems. Sometimes in our arrogance or ignorance, we are quick to offer solutions without knowing the full story. In the quoted bible verse, the serpent asked the question, already knowing the answer. But he framed the question in such a way

**Notes:**

as to lead Adam and Eve towards the destination he desired.

In our own lives today, we often lead ourselves into these traps, where we're not even asking the right questions, thus making our answers to those questions useless, or worse, harmful. But if we enter every encounter with respect and humility, we will learn just what the right questions are. Investing our time on the front end spares us the traps that arrogance might indeed have set for us. And thus, this approach benefits not only the client, but the consultant as well.

**Notes:**

# In-Flight:

"The heavens declare the glory of God." – Psalms 19:1

### *Glorious*

*Gray and White figures of every shape and size march towards your rising.*

*The darkness bows before you and the silence of morning awaits thee.*

*The night is washed away with strokes of Blue and Red.*

*How precious is each new day colored in hues of opportunity and redemption.*

*Glorious indeed.*

In those seasons when all is right within our family and our profession, might we sit in awe regarding how good our Creator has been to us. As

**Notes:**

we count our blessings and how undeserved favor has been poured out upon us, we are reminded of the eternal grace shown to each of us. Even though in truth, we know that we were being blessed during all of those times when we could not see the horizon, when we weren't flying high above the clouds.

So, let us praise God in the good times, bad times and all the times in between, if for no other reason than because our Creator is worthy of all our praises. "But even during the painful times?" you ask. Yes, even then.

Consider that all who were destined to be born into the flesh, are also destined to die in the flesh: be they worms, people, stars or all of creation. This is the nature of existence.

Thus, for the consultant, these truths provide perspective. Yes, we give our all each day to serve the needs of the client, but that cannot be all that our lives are about, not if we're people of faith. Life in the business world asks for many sacrifices from

**Notes:**

those of us who choose to be consultants. But be us ever mindful that our loved ones did not choose this life. And we too should be mindful that our Creator created us for more than the trappings and blessings of the consulting life. As we all well know, this can be a very demanding field: demanding of our energy and thoughts, but perhaps even more demanding of our time, particularly if we travel to our clients. It can be argued that time is our most precious gift. And often our life choices reflect just how precious this commodity is.

This is the reality of being a road warrior. However, let us not diminish or neglect our relationship with our Creator. Devotion to our Lord is much of what faith is about, and we must be intentional in this regard, for our own good. This is not to say that we need be dogmatic or pathological about it. If we pray in the evenings, and we drag ourselves to bed, then simply giving our Creator a quick shout out, "Lord…" will suffice (for God's Grace is sufficient). Same goes for those who do morning devotionals. As we say in the south, and it

**Notes:**

still is true, "The Lord knows my heart." Thus, praising and praying in all times, even when strapped for time, keeps us connected to our Source, and provides fuel and strength for when we encounter the turbulence which is certain to come. In this one regard, all of creation is equal.

**Notes:**

# Layover:

"When tempted, no one should say, 'God is tempting me.' For God cannot be tempted by evil, nor does God tempt anyone;" – James 1:13

*"The devil is not gonna come and get you, but he will meet you halfway."*

One could argue that when it comes to fidelity, as constant travelers we face no more temptation than those who don't travel for work. But there is one big difference. As road warriors we have far more opportunity to fall from grace (or as they say in the streets, "to get caught up in some foolishness"). And as any student of weekly crime shows has learned, misdeeds most often happen when motive meets opportunity.

As living breathing human beings, our senses

**Notes:**

can entice us. They're designed to do so. But as persons of faith who seek a higher truth, we are called to honor our commitments to each other, which obviously includes our loved ones back home.

However, for this part of our collective journey, as someone who has been a road warrior for nearly twenty-five years, I would like to offer some practical advice.

1) If possible, don't sit at the bar when out for dinner.

2) As a corollary to step one, either get your food to go, or get a table for one.

3) Don't step foot into a coworker's hotel room. Meet in the lobby if you need to connect after work hours.

4) Facebook is for old friends and people who are connected with you in some way (Church, School, etc…). LinkedIn is for folks

**Notes:**

you meet in your travels who you'd like to add to your network. For various reasons, LinkedIn has become a safe space to connect, if for no other reason than people seem to behave better when their professional lives could be negatively impacted. Facebook and the like, can be a less than positive experiences for those trying to stay the course, often with a healthy dose of negativity thrown in. So guard your spirit when in spaces like that.

5) Connecting with a group of coworkers after work for dinner is fine, as long as there are four or more of you meeting, and you've made your significant other aware of your plans.

6) As an extension to rule five, you shouldn't be connecting with anyone about whom you can't tell your significant other. If you have to hide it, you shouldn't be doing it.

7) Trust the Spirit within. If something doesn't

**Notes:**

feel right, it probably isn't, at least not for you. As my parents used to say to me, "Everything *ain't* for everybody."

**Notes:**

# Turbulence:

"But Jesus was sleeping. The disciples went to Jesus and woke him saying, 'Lord, save us! We're going to drown!'" – Matthew 8:24-25

*If the kingdom of heaven is indeed within us, might it be that challenges arise to awaken the God within us?*

It has been said, and still is true, that in every life rain must fall. The same is true for all of us frequent flyers. The Savings & Loan debacle, the Great Recession and a global pandemic were storms that were never in our plans. And some of the storms we face are more like microbursts that seemingly come out of nowhere, such as an unexpected job loss, divorce or a health crisis for yourself, or worse a loved one.

Regardless of the path taken, if we live long

**Notes:**

enough, we will find ourselves in a dinghy on a hostile sea with our God silent and seemingly asleep.

But God… Our God, is never far from us. In this faith we claim, our God is always with us; we only have to claim that which we already possess. God's Holy Spirit is able to carry us through any storm.  And mind you, as the world sees it, there may be little difference to others on the outside who are assessing our earthly situation.  But the transformation that the Holy Spirit provides blooms first within us, giving us a heavenly joy, which cannot be diminished by earthly circumstances. The Holy Spirit can provide us the peace and grace to calm any hostile sea, if only awakened.

**Notes:**

**Notes:**

# Service:

"God is not unjust; He will not forget the love that you have shown… " – Hebrews 6:10

### The Standard

*Sometimes you have to yield to the unreasonable, because of love. To go beyond that which appears just, is the very nature of love and mercy. But in the midst of doing this, do not lose sight of the One true Love; and balance all against this standard, regardless of what the expected outcome might be. May you always have faith enough to let go, and allow God.*

As servants of the Most-High, service to others is the central principle of whom we claim to be. But helping others on a consistent basis can be a real challenge when you're out of town five days a

**Notes:**

week, and even more so if you have a family (it's hard to spend your Saturday at the food bank when you haven't seen the family all week). I know this first hand because before I began consulting, I participated in a number of service activities. I served in each one before I met my wife, and continued after I got married. But once I started traveling in 1996, it became a real challenge. Over a period of time, it became clear that my old framework was no longer sustainable.

In short, the consulting life forced me to change how I served. It pushed me to doing things like homeless outreach on the weekends and leading small groups during the week after work. Also, plugging into existing service organizations, like Habitat for Humanity, can maximize the impact of one's service.

This spirit of being a help to my coworkers should extend into the workplace. Being territorial with knowledge is never a good practice, especially at someone else's company. We're there to make

**Notes:**

the project and the transformation outcome a success for the client, not to create fiefdoms. Bottomline, that's what we're being paid to do by the client. But on a more important level, we are ambassadors of our faith. Thus, we should do our best to model our Lord and Savior, who gave all.

**Notes:**

# Approach:

"Finally, all of you, be like minded, be sympathetic, love one another, be compassionate and humble." – 1 Peter 3:8

*If you cast your brother into the wilderness don't be surprised if he adapts.*

As outside consultants, we serve as change agents on behalf of our client. Our clients seek transformation through the process and technological changes we help them to implement. But generally speaking, human beings are resistant to change. Some resist because they see change as a threat to their position or power within a company. Others resist because they've become comfortable, and the process of changing is often uncomfortable. In fact, one could write a whole book on the barriers to change organizations typically face

**Notes:**

when attempting to transform.

There are a couple of things that I've found can ease the process for everyone. First, it is wise to approach the client's staff with a humble spirit. Listen to what they have to say. Consider their concerns regarding the proposed changes.

Secondly, as best you can, assure your client's staff that you're there to make their lives easier and more fruitful. Reassure them that you need their help and that you're there as a resource, to ensure that they'll be successful in the future state. And by walking with the staff through this transformation, we align with the client's staff, versus unwittingly setting up an 'us' versus 'them' scenario, where all parties lose.

But as people of faith, there is a greater truth. By modeling Christ, we will attract others to our

**Notes:**

Creator. By not always seeking our own way, those we encounter will see that we value them and what they have to contribute.

Fellow consultants, let us be ever mindful regarding how we speak to one another and the client. Let us strive to listen in love, and speak in the same way.

**Notes:**

# Landing:

"Therefore, go and make disciples of all nations, baptizing them in the name of the Father and of the Son and of the Holy Spirit." – Matthew 28:19.

*A truth unlived is a lie deeply rooted. But a truth purposely pursued, is a life in full bloom.*

When the sun hangs low, and we look out over our fields, what shall we say?

The good gardener plants trees whose fruit she may never taste, and seeds for crops she may never harvest. Truth is, this is what Christ did for each of us. Thus, we are called to grow where we're planted. And although we often quote the Great Commission, shown above, my Bible scholar friends tell me that a more accurate translation is, "As you go along, make disciples of all nations, baptizing them in the name of the Father, and of the

**Notes:**

Son and of the Holy Spirit." A subtle difference, but one which is very germane to this discussion. It's a difference which speaks to us ministering where we're planted. Thus, we don't need to get on a plane, train or car to share God's love. For if we allow God to shine through wherever we're planted, we will draw all men and women unto the One who first called us. So, when we're on the client site, let us be careful to guard our witness, so that we do not in any way diminish the Kingdom of God.

**Notes:**

# Taxying:

"Gentle words bring life and health; a deceitful tongue crushes the spirit." – Proverbs 15:4.

*Measure your words like the treasure they are, for with each one, you pour out a bit of your soul.*

In the workplace it can be difficult to watch a teammate struggle with work or in their personal life. Difficulties in life can be as common as breathing. And each time we face them, our God is near. Thus, sometimes it is our destiny to be their point of contact with God's grace. It's not that we're called to offer them a sermon. No, what we most often have to offer in the workplace is our patience, our understanding, and the grace that was so freely shared with us. And as we all know, in the near term, sometimes things don't work out. But we

**Notes:**

must have faith enough to trust in God's larger plans. Thus, when we see a teammate, whether working for the client or not, struggle to the point of separation, let us be encouragers, offering words of encouragement as they move through their own personal storm.

Let us not forget, that not a single one of us, has not been blessed to have someone reach out to us in our time of need. The Lord has sent these angels, to show grace to us, speak life into us or even to walk with us. We who are called to serve the Lord, are called to be that buoy on a rough sea, that guiding voice in the darkness or even that hand reaching down into the pit.

Please keep in mind that most often you are only one of the angels your teammate will encounter, but sometimes, rare though they may be, you are indeed the only angel in their time of need, as was the Good Samaritan.

**Notes:**

# Disembarking:

"Though you have not seen Him, you love Him. Though you do not see Him, you believe in Him and rejoice in a joy that is inexpressible and filled with glory." – 1 Peter 1:8

*The Secrete Sorrow of Saints*

*It's not the going without.*

*It's not the standing firm through any season.*

*It's not risking prison and torture for a belief.*

*It's not offering one's own life as a living sacrifice.*

*It's not even the suffering they bear on behalf of those they'll never know.*

*It's the sorrow they feel for those of us*

**Notes:**

*who will never know the love, joy and contentment*

*of being completely one with the Lord.*

*To give one's self over totally to the Author of our existence*

*is an unspeakable joy, which causes every saint to weep*

*because they cannot convey it in words or deeds.*

*They can only point the way,*

*for it is both universal and singular,*

*and can only be experienced within our own tears.*

When our lives near their end, what shall we say when we look back over our lives? When we step onto our last gangway, when we close our laptops and when we unpack our bags for the last time, what evidence of us will there be, beyond our own households? Sure, taking care of our family is

**Notes:**

an unspeakable blessing, but is that the only call God places on our lives?

Might I offer a thought for your consideration? Perhaps our most distinctive ministry lies outside of our homes, in small everyday moments. Though surely the Lord wants us to care for our families and tithe as we are able. But, might it also be true that the Lord smiles the most at our free will offerings? When we stop to help those in need, when we forgo evening workouts to help a team member who's struggling or we simply hold our tongue when someone we encounter is not ready for the truth.

It is said that even bad men love their mothers. Thus, we must ask ourselves, should ministry literally stop at our own front doors? Meaning, that this faith walk offers us so much more, if we only dare to pursue it. The ones we call saints and mystics of true faith knew that we've only scratched the surface when we first accept our salvation. And I get it, sometimes we hesitate to go

**Notes:**

deeper into our faith, because we're afraid, that the Lord will ask too much of us. But two points come to mind to contest this thought. First, all of our time, energy and life belong to God anyway. Secondly, as we grow in faith, walking in faith becomes easier. So today, I'm not asking you to sell all your belongings and eat only roots and berries for the rest of your earthly life. But I am asking you to trust our Creator when asked to step just a little bit further into this great sea we call faith.

**Notes:**

# Baggage Claim:

"Forgive one another, just as in Christ God forgave you."
– Ephesians 4:32

*Only those things which you hold on to, can bind you.*

In life and in work, we will be hurt. People and situations will seemingly move against you, sometimes even with willful intent. And honestly, it's not always what happened, but what we perceive to be the motivation behind the action which really hurts us. The pain is real. In the workplace these "attacks," as we see them, can threaten our tenure with the client, and sometimes even our careers. But if we have faith, who can deny us what God has intended for us? That's right, no one!

**Notes:**

But in the moment, it can be hard to see this truth, and even more so to feel it. Sometimes, we have conflicts which are subjective in nature; other times, it's clear from an objective perspective that we were definitely wronged. Regardless, the remedy is the same, we must forgive them. As followers of Christ, this is what we're required to do. To be clear, forgiveness doesn't mean not holding others accountable, nor does it mean we should remain in hostile situations, any more than one should remain in an abusive relationship. However, there's a season for everything, and sometimes for your best interest and that of your family, you must move on. And yet, we must forgive, as we are called to do. This forgiveness that we offer is not for the one with whom we are in conflict. No, it is for our own benefit. For our Creator knows how unforgiveness weighs on us and drags us down. Living in Grace means not being bound by things from our past. This forgiveness asked of us extends even to forgiving ourselves,

**Notes:**

once we've placed it on the altar. To serve our Lord more fully, we must let go of those things which bind us.

**Notes:**

# A Place to Stay:

"My Father's house has many rooms; if that were not so, would I have told you that I am going there to prepare a place for you? ³ And if I go and prepare a place for you, I will come back and take you to be with me that you also may be where I am." – John 14:2-3

*Open Up Your Eyes*

*Open your eyes and see that your destiny lies not within the chains of your past.*
*Open your eyes and see that this is just a moment and will not last.*
*Open your eyes and see the limits are only the ones you set.*
*Open your eyes and see, the barriers are only the ones you accept.*

*If you are of the Spirit of all creation, how can*

**Notes:**

*anything or anyone diminish that reflection? If you are of the hands of the Creator, what marvels in all the earth and sky are any greater?*

*Open your eyes and see, humility before God is the key to every door.*
*Open your eyes and see, that your life is not your own, but the Creator's.*
*Open your eyes and see, the Creator's love for you through me.*
*Open your eyes and see, your life as it was meant to be.*

In over twenty years of weekly travel, there have been times that I forgot to make a reservation, but not once have I gone without a room and bed to lay my head. Everything I have needed; my God has provided. Our Creator, before we were born, before the creation of this level of existence, knew us. Our God knew everything about us, what we'd do right, what we'd do wrong and everything in

**Notes:**

between. And yet, Christ has promised room for each of us in the Kingdom of Heaven. In fact, if we are in Christ Jesus, then we are already home. For the Kingdom of Heaven lives within each of us once we accept God into our hearts.

Therefore, worry for nothing. All that is to be, has already been written. Be there a question with your family or your job, arrangements have already been made for you. This doesn't mean that the path to your destiny will be straight as the world sees it, but it is your destiny nonetheless: every paycheck, every promotion, every separation, every opportunity, every encounter, every scar, every homegoing and every birth. For by God's grace, we've been allowed a role in the grand plan. Even when we were lost, it was written that we would be found. For while we were still in the world, Christ Jesus remembered us.

**Notes:**

# Day One:

"Do not be conformed to this world, but be transformed by the renewal of your mind, that by testing you may discern what is the will of God, what is good and acceptable and perfect." – Romans 12:2

*The false faith of fear binds, but true Faith frees us to become all that God has for us.*

Emotionally, the hardest day of any new assignment with a new client is the first day on the job. But if we start our day with a devotion and draw nearer to God, then we will by that process, as much as we allow, be filled with the Holy Spirit. In doing so, we will have a measure of grace that we can call on throughout our work day.

So just what does that look like? It means once we're done with our morning prayer, letting

**Notes:**

go and trusting God to provide all our needs. It means focusing on the tasks of the day. Day one activities typically involve getting up to speed on the client's needs. You're not going to retain it all between those two ears of yours on the day one; so focus more on your sources of information. Who are the living, breathing repositories of knowledge? These wells of information will be your life blood when you start up, but will also likely be many of the same people you'll pour into as the project proceeds, and your allies as you attempt to transform your client.

This lesson is also applicable in our lives outside of the work place. Having faith in God does not absolve us from doing our part. But it does promise that if we do our part, our Lord in heaven will be there to assure that all things work together for our good. For in truth, each day which we arise is a new day, day one of the rest of our lives, filled with opportunities to walk with our Lord and Savior. For though all these earthly things will pass away, our relationship with our Creator, the Holy

**Notes:**

Spirit, is eternal.

**Notes:**

# The Work:

"And let us not grow weary of doing good, for in due season we will reap, if we do not give up." – Galatians 6:9

*If a gust can sway your path, perhaps it was never yours to walk. Destiny is a state of being, not a destination.*

In the workplace after all the introductions and initial information gathering, it's time to go to work. It's what we do. The work is the work, and yet this phase (i.e. the Build Phase) can be the most tranquil time during a project. Although challenges do arise during this phase, we are empowered to overcome each impediment. It's the very reason that we are with the client.

Likewise, in our spiritual lives, we are called to serve God in the Kingdom of Heaven. From this holy fountain within us, the Creator's Holy Spirit

**Notes:**

flows through us, that we might serve our God's divine will. Whether it be in the music ministry, feeding the homeless, nurturing the spiritual development of those around us or wherever.

Even though we know that there will be false starts and setbacks, God calls us to persist, to have faith. If you believe that you are called to a thing, then do not let your faith waiver. For just because we are called to a field, it does not mean that the work will be easy. But what is promised is that our labors will bear fruit, whether we live to see it or not. In this life, rare is the gardener who sees the harvest from every seed planted.

And to this point, in my own life God called me to write, and put writing this devotion on my heart. Yet, I must concede that I resisted. It's one thing to write works of fiction, and quite another to reveal one's own heart and be fully transparent (search me Lord), that the Truth might be shared. Although I am older now, the fire that first started all those years ago still burns. Like so many people,

**Notes:**

during my walk with God, I've been called to serve in many areas, and yet writing this book has been something I've wrestled with for nearly seventeen years now.

**Notes:**

# Conflict:

"Know this, my beloved brothers. Let every person be quick to hear, slow to speak, slow to anger." James 1:19

*Do not sow anger, lest you reap a harvest of destruction.*

      Each of us has a story of workplace conflict. Despite our best efforts, moments or even seasons of conflict will find us in the workplace. And as consultants, we are often the agents of change that our client has brought in to facilitate enterprise-wide transformation. As we all learned in Change Management 101, human beings are often resistant to change. Given that people process their fears and concerns in different ways, some do so by being obstinate or difficult, while others may actively work to sabotage your efforts.

**Notes:**

And while this devotional is about seeking personal development in Christ, I'd like to offer the best means I've found to lessen resistance to change. If possible, pull as many stakeholders as practical into the change management process during the planning phase. For when people have an opportunity to voice their thoughts during the planning phase, they know that they've been heard, regardless of whether or not the team goes with their suggestions. Thus, from the design to implementation, they're more likely to be on board and working with you, rather than against you.

Yet despite your best change management efforts, conflicts will still come your way. But as with much of life in or outside of the workplace, it's not what happens to you, but rather how we respond. For our response is the only thing which we can control when these squalls rise up. As people of faith, we are called to measure our words, and not to strike out in anger. We are called to let God fight our battles. That means that we must be

**Notes:**

Christ centered, especially in times of conflict. In these moments, we must remember who we are, and represent so. Does this mean that we can't defend ourselves? No, not at all. But it does mean that we are not to return wrong for wrong, for if we do, we will surely reap what we sow.

**Notes:**

# Stepping Back:

"A fool gives full vent to his spirit, but a wise man quietly holds back." – Proverbs 29:11

*In this mortal life the only constant is change. Booms and recessions come and go. In our professional lives we seek to sow when times are good, and adjust when the market is soft. Our goal is to always take it all in stride.  And yet sometimes it seems, change goes beyond the pale.*
*But never forget, though the winds of turmoil come and go, professionally and personally, we have an anchor which holds firm.*

Sometimes, even professionally, we can be too close to a situation or moment to see it clearly. In a given moment when we're blindsided, for a second we can lose our balance. However, we

**Notes:**

should always take a beat before saying anything. For not every assertion, accusation or proclamation deserves a response, much less an instant one. The holding of one's tongue (or response to an email or text), is often the best path professionally. Very rarely must we enter the realm of professional combat hastily, if ever. I would even argue that pretty much every bad decision that I have made was made in haste. Again, not everything needs a response. In fact, often by just sitting back, things will play out for the common good.

On a personal level I've come to understand much the same. I realize that sometimes I've done more harm by saying what's on my mind, even when I've been right, with those I love. As a man, my inclination was always to try to "fix" things. But sometimes folks just want to vent, cry or scream, and rather than debate them or try to "fix" them or the situation, I've found it better to step back and not engage. Often, after some time has passed and some healing has come, we can then have a more productive conversation. And if that conversation

**Notes:**

never happens, I need to be okay with that too, I need to be okay, with not getting the last word in.

Again, that is my walk, my discovery, and I hope that it resonates with you as well. We all want to be heard, but before we speak, we must consider if the ground in which we wish to plant our seeds is fertile? For if it is not, then our breath is wasted. Better to await the Holy Spirit to guide us, even if that means holding our tongue indefinitely.

**Notes:**

# Presentation:

"Keep your conduct among the Gentiles honorable, so that when they speak against you as evildoers, they may see your good deeds and glorify God on the day of Visitation." 1 Peter 2:12

*Wisdom is less about being right or wrong, than knowing when to speak and when to remain silent.*

As consultants, presentation typically refers to the act of showing our work to the client, be it a formal presentation, system test results, or whatever. But as people of faith, it can have a another meaning as well. As Christians, often we are charged to "guard our witness." This means that all times we must be ethical, kind hearted, not ones to pass along gossip, and generally to behave in a

**Notes:**

way that does not besmirch the love of Christ. We do this so that should a moment arise when we must share our testimony regarding our Faith, we have the standing to do so.

I say this because whether you're conscious of it or not, those around you are always watching and taking note of what you say and do. While this can take many forms, it is my personal belief that we are at most risk of damaging our witness by what we say. For it is said that "the power of life and death is held in the tongue." When we speak of others in an un-Christ like fashion, we damage our ability to witness for Christ. When we say witness, we most often think of when we are called to give our testimony when leading someone to Christ. But don't you know that we are witnessing for Christ with every encounter, every word we speak and even the words we don't say!

Know this too, that some are called to plant, others to water, and a few to harvest. In other words, you may not actually see the fruit of your

**Notes:**

labor, particularly in a mobile society like ours. But do not let this diminish your joy of serving, or deter you from sharing God's love each and every day.

**Notes:**

# Uncertain Times:

"For I know the plans I have for you, declares the Lord, plans for your welfare and not for evil, to give you a future and a hope." Jeremiah 29:11

*Faith empowers us to thrive, in spite of the uncertainty all around us. It is the Light within us, which illuminates our destiny*

I learned a valuable lesson early on in my career, and that is, in the modern era, there is no such thing as job security. I entered the professional workforce during the last big recession before the "Great Recession" in the late 1980's. At that time many companies were either right sizing or downsizing. Regardless, it made for a difficult job market. The other shift during that time was the move away from pensions to employee-owned

**Notes:**

401K's. One employer for which I'd worked nearly five years, during a rightsizing initiative, called me down to HR to let me know that I would be keeping my position managing conversion projects. And while I was pleased to hear that, being newly married, I'd already begun looking for other opportunities well before that proclamation. I accepted a position with another firm, making 5 to 10k more per year. But the enduring takeaway I took from the choppy employment waters of the late eighties and early nineties, was that job security was fool's gold. All of this opened me to the possibility of being a consultant. For if, in actuality I was taking on risk, for which I was not being compensated, might I not be better off earning more as a consultant? In my simple mind, both paths carried significant risk; thus, it made sense to become a consultant.

Professionally, it also taught me how to perform in the midst of uncertainty, which is the reality of this profession that we've chosen. The job market turmoil of the time was more than a

**Notes:**

professional lesson; it was also life lesson.

Certainty is an illusion, for there is no certainty in life, never was, never will be. These two facts are the bookends of fear. We close our minds because we crave certainty, but it is a fool's quest. It is better that we learn how to press on despite our fears. For if we give into fear, and close our own minds, we may well become the very thing that we fear.

In my faith tradition, we call this walking by faith. And dare I say that if I am never uncomfortable, then I must ask myself whether I am truly exercising my Faith.

Bottomline, we must walk in our faith and our destiny, as we workout our salvation. For our destiny is less a destination, and more a state of being.

**Notes:**

# Feedback:

"Listen to advice and accept instruction, that you may gain wisdom in the future."
Proverbs 19:20

*"Don't cut your nose off to spite your face."* —
*Mama.*

If the truth be told, I skated through high school. I pretty much never needed to study outside of class, since I got most of my homework assignments done during study hall. I just had to pay attention during class, and got it. The lone exceptions were book reports. I struggled with them (oh, the irony), not because I had any trouble comprehending them. No, it was more of an issue of me being a first-class procrastinator. Seemingly without fail, I'd wait until the Friday evening before the Monday when my book report was due,

**Notes:**

to get serious about the assignment. But otherwise, I just sat in class, paid attention and passed my tests.

Thankfully, a handful of my teachers, held me to a higher standard. They were hard on me, because they knew what the world beyond those walls required, and they loved me enough to challenge me, to apply a finer eye to the work I turned in. In the moment, it threatened my self-perception of being a smart young man. But they saw what I could be, or better put, they saw what I needed to be. These teachers not only offered me a foretaste of what adult life required, they also, showed me what greater love looks like. Holding me accountable was how they showed love for me.

And so, it is in the workplace and in our professions. Let us not be so prideful as to not be willing to listen to constructive criticism, be it in regards to how much detail we go into during our presentation, being the first one in and one of the last to leave when hosting a meeting, or even what

**Notes:**

clothing is appropriate in the workplace (side note: dress codes vary by industry and region, so always overdress day one; so that you can see what their dress code is in practice). Thus, humble yourself, and listen to those who pull you aside and offer heartfelt feedback. In the end, you (and The Lord) are the master of your own ship. Still, you should never dismiss feedback from those you respect without serious consideration.

**Notes:**

# Coaching:

"Iron sharpens Iron, and one man sharpens another." Proverbs 27:17

*"Drawing lines in the sand is a waste of time, for with each passing wave, our position erodes."*

As we work to provide value for our clients, let us be mindful of those still trying to find their way. There is a tendency in our profession for people to hold on to information and spaces (what I call *anti-coaching*). We are often tempted to protect our positions, and in our fields that translates into an unwillingness to share what we know.  While I understand that motivation, I've strived not to be that guy. First off, I'm there to provide value to the client, not to build my own kingdom. So, I'm open to sharing knowledge and skills with not only the client's staff, but also with my fellow consultants,

**Notes:**

even if they're at that client through a different firm.

Secondly, if we're all there to assist the client in transforming into what they wish to be, which is ultimately what they're paying us for, then we should all be pulling the same way. Put another way, at my first programming job out of undergrad the director told us, the new crop of programmers on day one, "The day you become indispensable, is the day that I fire you." He was saying that the moment you become "that guy," you're done. Simply put, we should always be of a mind to coach one another up.

Much of this is applicable to our lives as believers, outside of church as well. We are called to build the kingdom of heaven together. For what good does it do me to feast at God's table, if my brother and sister who I love, aren't sitting beside me? Therefore, do I not only have the responsibility to share Godly knowledge with others, but also to speak hard truths and to lovingly hold others in my

**Notes:**

personal circle accountable. And while the how we might accomplish this may differ between home and work, it can still be done. And yes, challenging those we love can be uncomfortable, but we weren't promised to a life of comfort when we first accepted our call. In fact, we were actually called to move forward, despite our discomfort. That's kind of the point of faith, isn't it?

Thus, we must show those who come behind us what active faith looks like. And by allowing our loved ones to see how we handle adversity is the most effective coaching any parent, sibling or friend can share.

**Notes:**

# Bench Time:

"When He sent them away, He went up onto a mountain by himself to pray. Evening came, and He was still alone." Matthew 14:23

*"If we can but turn a blind eye to ourselves, we might see the whole world."*

Bench Time is the time between assignments, when you're still gainfully employed but you're in the office or at home, preparing for the next gig, or if you're an independent consultant you're taking a sabbatical or another form of planned time off. Regardless of your situation, you are, to varying degrees, free from the rigors of the consulting life and the challenges of life on the road. It's opportunity to spend quality time with your family, as you try to make up for being gone so much. And

**Notes:**

although, nothing can fully replace the time we were away, we certainly do try, by making ourselves ultra-available. It's a natural and thoughtful response. This behavior is common among those who travel weekly or even daily in how we seek to make up for loss family time. And personally, I know that I use these breaks to connect with siblings, cousins and friends (I'm the let's do lunch king). And yet, from a professional perspective, we need to use these times of lessened activity to recharge, for our own well-being. These mental and physical breaks can make us better at whatever we do.

For many consultants, bench time, especially when planned in advance, can be more than time to rest up and look inward. It can also be an opportunity to look outwardly to your community. There are always needs, and as many of you know, it's hard to participate in any sort of regular ministry when you're on the road so much. When I got married nearly thirty years ago, I was a regular volunteer in several ministries via my church home.

**Notes:**

However, when I hit the road as a consultant in 1996, my ability to participate in these various activities diminished greatly. One by one, I pulled back from these ministries, as the time I did have on the weekends at home was focused on my immediate family. I'm sure that many of you can relate to this experience. Yes, consulting has been and still is a blessing in so many ways, but it comes with a price.

And yet, if we are intentional, we can plan activities which serve the blessed community. If we're home for the holidays, we can schedule our entire household to serve meals at a local shelter or food pantry. Or, if so led, perhaps participate in mission work. The point being, if you are filled with a heart to serve, you will find opportunities to do so, if you seek them.

**Notes:**

# In the Wilderness:

"At once the Spirit sent him out into the wilderness, and he was in the desert forty days..." Mark 1:12

*"Looking back can be healthy, but going back is not what this life is about."*

Despite our best efforts, there will come a time when we will find ourselves in the wilderness. These are times when the leads dry up, technology moves past us, or the economy craters. In these times, the first instinct is to look back to perhaps see where we went wrong, or what we could have done differently. But if I may, I'd like to offer a word of caution. Look back only enough to inform your path forward. Don't consume the past whole. Take only from the past what you need, and leave the rest behind, so that you remain nimble and agile in your thinking and your actions. Often when change happens, those who are still gnawing on the

**Notes:**

past find themselves stuck in it. The biggest trait of successful people is their ability to accept change.

Likewise, on a spiritual basis, we can also find ourselves adrift. Some call these tests of faith, the dark night of the soul. All who've spent any significant period of time on this third rock from the sun, will face hard times at some point in their lives. And if you haven't yet, just keep on living and you will. As people of faith, we are taught to "just hold on to Jesus." Yes, that is the core of who we are, but I think too, that our Lord wants us to, in business terms, manage change. By that I mean that we must give over whatever sense of loss (divorce, a death in the family, job loss, etc…) we're still hanging on to, to our Creator, so that we can move forward towards who we are becoming. Our Creator has a plan and a destiny for each of us, and it is a plan for our good. And know too, that this transformation, this salvation each of us is called to workout, is not always in terms that others in the flesh can see. But trust and believe any who are in the light, will see that same light within you as

**Notes:**

well.

Lastly, let's be clear, our time in the wilderness, should not be wasted in self-pity. No, even as with our Savior, time in the wilderness, is an opportunity to reassess our lives and priorities, and to deepen our commitment and faith. It can be, if we allow it, a time of transformation.

**Notes:**

# Letting Go:

"Let all bitterness and wrath and anger and clamor and slander be put away from you, along with all malice. Be kind to one another, tenderhearted, forgiving one another, as God in Christ forgave you." Ephesians 4:31-32

*Letting the wind blow & the fire rage.*

*Allowing in the pain, allowing it free reign.*

*Allowing it to twist & turn, allowing it to blister & burn.*

*Trying not to be, that I might become.*

Though most of us have a passion for our chosen profession, it can be a mental and physical grind, that takes a toll on our bodies and our families. And beyond that, broadly speaking, it's a

**Notes:**

fast-moving field, which can quickly pass one by if one does not actively cultivate his or her skillset. As markets shift, one should do one's best to anticipate the changes coming, and tilt one's sails accordingly. In short, regarding our careers, one must be quick to accept the truth of things, and often that means letting go of the current state.

Likewise, in our personal and spiritual lives, we must also note which way the winds are blowing. For although remaining as we are or where we are, is usually the most comfortable thing in the moment, remaining where we are personally and spiritually, can lead to unwanted outcomes in our lives. In short, I'm suggesting that we be spiritually grounded, and at the same time, be personally and mentally flexible.

For instance, the harsh reality is that if we are blessed to live long enough, we'll eventually need to leave our two-story family home and find a smaller home, with a first-floor master (only so many miles on these knees, y'all). Thus, we need

**Notes:**

not be wedded to any physical object, not even our home. But letting go can be the hardest of things to do, especially when we're angry. Yet our lives our lives outside of work may bring us even harder things that we must let go. It might be a spouse through separation, divorce or death. Or perhaps a child who we assess to be wayward, who will not listen to the lessons we've learned. We must learn to let go, (grieving however we must) so that we can move on to whatever God has next for us, and so that others can move on as well. I know for sure that our Creator did not create us to stand still, for all of Creation testifies to this fact. Or in others words, in the most devastating moments, we have no choice but turn over situations, people, all of it over to God. For some burdens can only be carried by God alone.

**Notes:**

# Packing Up:

"There is a time for everything, and a season for every activity under heaven: a time to be born and a time to die, a time to plant and a time to uproot." Ecclesiastes 3:1-3

*"Our souls long for that which the flesh dreads, when our Creator calls us home. For each of us, a day awaits with our name upon it. It's impossible to see, but it will be found."*

Even though some contracts seem as though they will never end, they all do, eventually. We know the routine, turn over all pertinent documentation and how-to guides, so that once we're gone, our deeds and our instructions endure. Sure, we'll no longer expect any more payments from our clients, but in loving what we do, and being passionate about our profession, we want the best for our clients. So, before we close our laptops

**Notes:**

for the final time, we share our contact information, speak words of encouragement to those who need to hear it and pack up one last time leaving our workstation as we found it.

The same is true in our personal lives. Indeed, no engagement is eternal, for there is a day with our name upon it for each of us who take breath. Thus, as adults who accept the reality of what is and what is to come, we must plan accordingly. Yes, we want to assess things like life insurance, long term care, wills and trusts, we are all much more than the trappings of wealth we seek to preserve and pass on. Our real legacy is how we lived our lives. Those around may or may not remember the words we've said, but they will always remember the things that we did, and more accurately, how those actions made them feel. Thus, let us ask for forgiveness from anyone we may have hurt, regardless of who was right and who was wrong.

**Notes:**

In addition, if we are able, let us settle old accounts. Let us forgive those who may have wronged us. And in those matters, where we cannot address the matter with the relevant parties because we've lost contact, or those parties have gone on to glory already, may we let go, and give it all over to our Lord. And truth be told, since we don't know the day nor the hour when we will return to our Lord, let us be mindful to settle our accounts as soon as we realize that we are in debt. Let us be quick to forgive and quick to speak words of life into one another because we may not get a second chance to do so.

**Notes:**

# Exit Interview:

"Now faith is the substance of things hoped for, the evidence of things not seen."
Hebrews 11:1

*"It's not about where you started or the destination. It's about the Journey."*

As consultants, from the client's perspective, we are hired to someday be terminated (note that I don't say fired). For when our purpose to our client comes to an end, so does our contract. It is a fact of business for which we must prepare. Although sometimes engagements end abruptly, typically we have the opportunity to say our goodbyes. If we are especially blessed, we may even be offered an exit interview, even if it's just an informal conversation as we celebrate another successful project. Now, that it's all done, what does the client think of the

**Notes:**

results and our ability to guide them towards the transformation they sought when they first engaged us?

Likewise, in our own lives, none of us knows the day nor the hour, when we will be called home to the One above all. But we all know that someday we will be called home. And on that day, what shall we say before the Lord? Will we be able to give a good account? Will God be pleased with the fruit of our labor, our sacrifice? For if we are believers, beyond our personal salvation, our goal in this life is to live in a way that our lives are a sweet-smelling offering to the Lord.

**Notes:**

# The Harvest:

"I am the true vine, and my Father the vinedresser." John 15:1

*"The Good Gardener plants crops that they will never harvest."*

      We book the flights, we walk the concourses, we eat the dinners in our laps thirty thousand feet above the ground, and stepping into unfamiliar spaces we get comfortable with being uncomfortable. We have a love for reason that surpasses most, and yet we strive to be humble before our clients, that they might truly hear us and know that we have their best interest at heart. Being the external force, we take extra care to be respectful in someone else's home. And yet, when it's time to deliver the truth of things, we do so without fear or favor. For knowledge and reason are the tools of our trade, and the corner stone of any

**Notes:**

home that we help build. We are reasoned people who are internally driven to do good work. And yet, despite it all, most often we are long gone by the time the fruits of our labor are harvested.

Likewise, in our personal lives, the fruit of much of what we may plant may not blossom until we are long gone from this world. The love that we pour into our spouses, children, grandchildren, other family and friends, will bear fruit in due season. We may be blessed, in season, to see some of what we've sown, when it is reaped. But if we are indeed good gardeners, the fields we plant will continue to produce crops which are rich in God's Holy Spirit long after we've returned to our creator. Our actions, the things we say and even the things we don't say, all bear witness to God's love. For even as we share love here, we know that through the love of the Holy Spirit, those who came before us passed along God's word and God's Spirit to us. Thus, we strive to do the same.

Gifts of the Spirit abound all around us.

**Notes:**

# The Way:

"Jesus answered, "I am the way, the truth, and the life. No one comes to the Father except through me." John 14:6

*"I am the thorn in your crown, the mark on your back and the hole in your side, and still, you bless me."*

Everyday, I fail to live up to the call you placed on my heart so long ago. And every night Lord I lay down adrift in my fears.

And still, You hold me.

Time and time again, I stray from your pasture, to roam the darkness.

And still, You find me.

I fall daily, stiff necked as I am, not seeing the

**Notes:**

stones before me, the very stones You said would obstruct my path.

And still, You lead me…

There are no words which truly capture the measure of Your love, no words at all. The mountains before me are high, and the valleys beside me are deep. And yet, You set a path for me, that I might know the Way back to You.

Blessed is your word. Blessed is your love.

Lord, your grace and mercy are unspeakable gifts to all. Before we were born and before the pillars of the earth were set, you offered them to us. It is my earnest prayer that I and all who call your name would go into this world to share the love you've poured into us.

**Thank You, Lord…**

**Notes:**

**Notes:**

**Notes:**

**Notes:**

**Notes:**

**Notes:**

**Notes:**

**Notes:**

**Notes:**

**Notes:**

**Notes:**